The *State Museum* of Pennsylvania

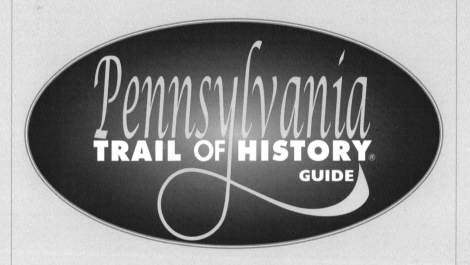

Pennsylvania
TRAIL OF HISTORY®
GUIDE

Text by Sharon Hernes Silverman

STACKPOLE BOOKS

PENNSYLVANIA HISTORICAL
AND MUSEUM COMMISSION

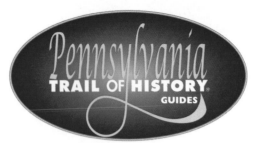

Kyle R. Weaver, Series Editor
Tracy Patterson, Designer

Published by
STACKPOLE BOOKS
5067 Ritter Road
Mechanicsburg, Pennsylvania 17055

Printed in the United States of America
2 4 6 8 10 9 7 5 3 1
FIRST EDITION

Maps by Caroline Stover

All photographs are from the collection
of The State Museum of Pennsylvania

Library of Congress Cataloging-in-Publication Data

Silverman, Sharon Hernes.
    The State Museum of Pennsylvania : Pennsylvania trail of history guide / Sharon Hernes Silverman.— 1st ed.
        p. cm.
    Includes bibliographical references and index.
    ISBN 0-8117-3214-2 (pbk. : alk. paper)
    1. State Museum of Pennsylvania—Guidebooks. 2. State Museum of Pennsylvania—History. 3. Pennsylvania—History—Sources. 4. Natural history—Pennsylvania—Sources. I. Title.

F146.5.S56 2005
974.8'18—dc22

2005003768

Contents

Editor's Preface

From the fossils of hundreds of millions of years ago to recent technological wonders, the Keystone State's past is preserved, exhibited, and interpreted at The State Museum of Pennsylvania. With collections too vast to ever hope to comprehensively cover in a guidebook of this size, the museum has chosen to highlight some of its treasures. The assortment is a balance of natural, social, cultural, and technological objects that represent the distinctive history of the state. Stackpole Books is pleased to continue its collaboration with the Pennsylvania Historical and Museum Commission (PHMC) to feature The State Museum in this new volume of the Pennsylvania Trail of History Guides.

Each book in the series focuses on one of the historic sites or museums administered by the PHMC. The series was conceived and created by Stackpole Books with the cooperation of the PHMC's Division of Publications and Bureau of Historic Sites and Museums. Donna Williams heads the latter, and she and her staff of professionals review the text of each guidebook for accuracy and have made many valuable recommendations. Diane Reed, Chief of Publications, has facilitated relations between the PHMC and Stackpole from the project's inception, organized the review process with the commission, and attended to numerous details related to the venture. The first people at the commission I spoke to in 1998, when I originally developed the idea for a series of Trail of History guidebooks, were site administrators Michael Ripton, formerly of Ephrata Cloister; Douglas A. Miller, of Pennsbury Manor; and James A. Lewars, of Daniel Boone Homestead. The guidance and encouragement these gentlemen offered to me led to discussions with the PHMC and the launching of the project.

At The State Museum, Director Anita Blackaby and Development Officer Beth Hager supported and encouraged the project from the start. Instrumental to the process were Howard Pollman, PHMC Marketing Director; William Sisson, Chief of the Curatorial Division; and Eric Ledell Smith, Historian. Smith's document, "The State Museum of Pennsylvania: A Centennial History, 1905–2005," provided the basis for the history chapter. The following museum personnel provided information or reviewed the text: Beatrice Hulsberg, Curator of Community and Domestic Life; Walter E. Meshaka, Jr., Senior Curator of Zoology and Botany; Curt Miner, Senior Curator of Popular Culture and Political History; N. Lee Stevens, Senior Curator of Fine Art; Robert M. Sullivan, Senior Curator of Paleontology and Geology; Stephen G. Warfel, Senior Curator of Archaeology; and John Zwierzyna, Senior Curator of Military and Industrial History.

The author of the text, Sharon Hernes Silverman, is a prolific journalist and expert on historic travel in Pennsylvania. She previously contributed to the series with the text for *Daniel Boone Homestead*. Here she writes about twenty treasures in the collection, from a dime-size trilobite fossil of the Paleozoic Era to an example of a remote operated vehicle used for cleaning up nuclear waste after the accident at Three Mile Island in 1979. Following this and a brief discussion of the evolution of the museum, Silverman concludes with a tour of the museum's exhibit halls and galleries.

Kyle R. Weaver, Editor
Stackpole Books

Introduction to the Site

Part of a museum's mission is to collect, safeguard, exhibit, and interpret relevant specimens and artifacts, and The State Museum of Pennsylvania fulfills this goal with singular distinction. Since 1905, the institution has preserved vast collections that chronicle the commonwealth's history and natural heritage from earth's beginning to the present. Today four floors of exhibits and activities bring this saga to life for museum visitors, examining and interpreting the state's archaeology and anthropology, native peoples, industry and technology, the legacy of William Penn, the Civil War, and much more.

An accreditation report issued by the prestigious American Association of Museums (AAM) in 1999 recognized The State Museum as "one of the nation's preeminent institutions of its kind." Rather than rest on these laurels, The State Museum is challenging itself to go beyond its traditional role, to look at itself not only as a steward of the past, but also as an advocate for Pennsylvania's people and, ultimately, their future. Along with collecting, preserving, and presenting specimens and artifacts, the museum supports the community through education and by addressing social issues.

To ensure its continued evolution, the museum invests time and money in education, best practices, technology, and exhibits. A digital planetarium, play-and-learn room for children, renovations to the building, and involvement of the staff with the larger museum world are just some of the many ways The State Museum of Pennsylvania is fulfilling its mission as it begins its second century.

Highlights of the Collection

The State Museum of Pennsylvania serves as the custodian for a wide variety of specimens and artifacts of importance to the natural and social history, culture, and people of Pennsylvania. The museum's collections include more than three million objects. Curators have identified the following items as highlights. Some are on long-term display; others are in storage for preservation purposes.

PHILLIPPE FLY ROD
The Phillippe fly rod is an extremely rare fishing implement made by gunsmith Samuel C. Phillippe (1801–77) of Easton, who is often credited with inventing the split-bamboo rod in America in 1846. This example features intricate carvings and engraving, a mother-of-pearl-decorated reel, and a velvet-lined mahogany storage case.

MINER'S HARD HAT, TOOL BELT, BATTERY-POWERED LAMP, AND LUNCH BUCKET

These items belonged to Marilyn Mc-Cusker of Coalport, Clearfield County, the first woman to be killed in a deep-mine accident in the United States. On October 2, 1979, she was the victim of a rockfall in the Rushton Mine near Osceola Mills, Centre County.

Ironically, about two years earlier, McCusker had been one of four women who filed a sex discrimination suit against Rushton Mining Company. The case was settled out of court. Terms of the settlement allowed the women to work underground and to receive back pay from the date on which they had applied to work in the mines.

KENTUCKY RIFLE

The Kentucky rifle was developed by German gunsmiths of southeastern Pennsylvania. It was adapted from the Old World jaeger hunting rifle for shooting game in the dense forests of America. This muzzleloader was a great improvement over the short, large-bore jaeger from which it evolved. Lengthening the barrel to forty inches or more increased the gun's range. A reduction in caliber meant that each ball of shot weighed less and required less powder. Parallel spiral grooves in the barrel caused the ball to spin, improving accuracy. The long, thin stock gave the rifle excellent balance and handling qualities. It weighed only seven to ten pounds, so it could be carried with one arm.

Although the gun originated in Pennsylvania, its manufacture spread to other states, including Maryland, Virginia, the Carolinas, and Ohio. The rifle acquired the name Kentucky after a ballad credited Andrew Jackson's rifle-toting Kentucky backwoodsmen with defeating the British at the 1815 Battle of New Orleans.

The rifle in The State Museum's collection was made by Christian Beck of Lebanon County about 1790. It features a curly maple stock, brass patchbox, and .50-caliber octagonal barrel.

ROVER

The ROVER, short for remote operated vehicle, was a device used in the cleanup after the 1979 Three Mile Island nuclear accident. Remotely operated through an umbilical cord, the ROVER has a camera and lights mounted on it, and had appendages that were used for handling contaminated materials. The ROVER used during cleanup was destroyed because it became contaminated during the operations. The museum's ROVER is a test model.

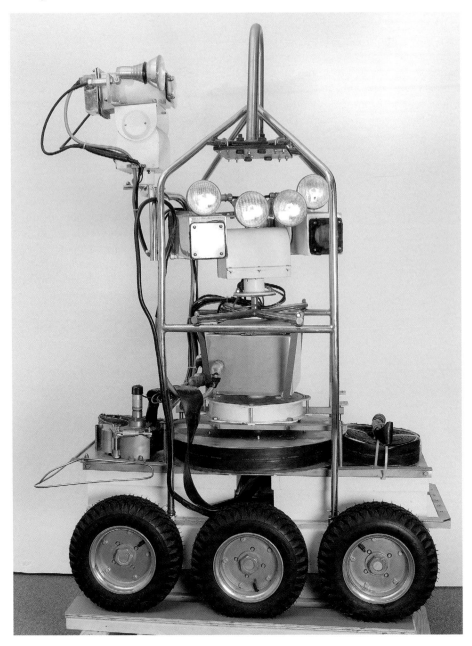

ALLIE TURNER'S DRUM
This drum belonged to Allie Turner,
reported to be the youngest drummer
in the Union Army during the Civil War.
Shortly after the war ended, Turner gave
the drum to the owner of the Railroad
Hotel in York, Pennsylvania, as payment
for food and lodging. The grandson of
the hotel owner donated the drum to
The State Museum in 1939. Turner may
have worked briefly for P. T. Barnum;
a photograph issued by the Barnum
Museum shows Turner with the drum.

USS *PENNSYLVANIA* SILVER SERVICE

In 1903, the Pennsylvania General Assembly appropriated $25,000 for an exquisite presentation silver service to be used aboard the newly constructed armored cruiser no. 4, the USS *Pennsylvania*. The assembly was following a tradition begun in the late nineteenth century, wherein states and towns presented silver services to their namesake naval vessels. The elaborately ornamented silver bore motifs and images to celebrate the achievements, history, traditions, and flora and fauna of the localities for which the ships were named. Proudly displayed in the officers' wardroom, the silver was used during ceremonies and special occasions.

The *Pennsylvania*'s service has 162 pieces containing nearly twelve thousand ounces of silver. It was produced under a contract with J. E. Caldwell & Company of Philadelphia. It documents in sterling the rich historical and natural heritage of Pennsylvania and includes symbols of the commonwealth's industrial accomplishments as well as images of prominent figures such as William Penn, John Dickinson, and David Rittenhouse. The state seal, nautical motifs, and native fauna such as elk, bears, and deer also adorn the silver service.

In 1916, the service was transferred to the newly commissioned battleship no. 38, the USS *Pennsylvania* (BB38). Just before World War II, the set was sent ashore for safekeeping. After the war, the *Pennsylvania* served as a target ship for the atomic bomb test at Bikini Atoll. In 1948, she was towed to sea and scuttled off Kwajalein. Meanwhile, in 1946, the silver

service was placed on the aircraft carrier USS *Valley Forge* (CV-45), which saw extensive action during the Korean conflict. In 1961, she was redesignated a helicopter landing ship (LPH-8), in which capacity she served until decommissioned in 1970. In the 1970s, the Navy loaned the silver service to the Pennsylvania Historical and Museum Commission; in 1998, at the request of Gov. Tom Ridge, the Navy granted full and permanent title to the commonwealth.

PENNSYLVANIA GERMAN *SCHRANK*

This *schrank* (*Kleiderschrank* roughly translates to "clothes press") is an outstanding example of eighteenth-century cabinetmaking. Made of native walnut decorated with inlay composed of molten sulfur, it probably came from a workshop in Manheim, Lancaster County. The names "I H Kauffmann" and "A N Kauffmann" appear on the door panels, along with the German phrase "D I Mertz," which refers to the first of March, and the year 1766.

This piece was most likely made for the Kauffmanns' wedding. The *schrank* was a necessary piece of furniture for storing clothing and textiles, as closets were not normally part of a house during this period. The interior is divided, with shelves on the left side and pegs on the right.

Schranks, large and heavy, were constructed so that they could be taken apart for moving. The Kauffmann *schrank* adds to our understanding of eighteenth-century Pennsylvania German culture through its craftsmanship and design motifs.

STAR OF BETHLEHEM QUILT

Bursting with color, this quilt was made between 1890 and 1920 in West Hanover Township, Dauphin County. The Pennsylvania German influence is unmistakable. The meticulously pieced top was made by Sally Albright and the elaborate stitching was done by a Mrs. Moyer, who was nicknamed "Quilt Moyer" for her expertise.

The unusual pumpkin-colored fabric is an outstanding choice for the background. Double pink fabric is used in the sawtooth border, smaller stars, and within the large star. Printed fabrics in black, blue, and yellow complete the palette of the star, which appears to float above the background.

The top was hand stitched and the border machine sewn. Quilting was done by hand, with seven stitches per inch in feather, diamond, and floral patterns. The cotton fabrics, purchased new for this quilt, have maintained their vibrant colors, and the quilt is in excellent condition. A superb specimen, this is an example of the importance and long history of textile work in Pennsylvania.

MARY BEAVER'S INAUGURAL BALL GOWN

Mary Allison McAllister married James Addams Beaver, future governor of Pennsylvania, on December 26, 1865. Beaver was a partner in McAllister's father's law firm in Bellefonte, Centre County, and he had served with honor and distinction for the Union during the Civil War.

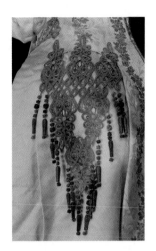

He was elected governor of Pennsylvania in 1886, having been active in state and national politics for many years.

The gown, worn by Mrs. Beaver at her husband's inaugural ball, was donated to The State Museum of Pennsylvania in 1965 by her granddaughter Margaret B. Wilkinson. Its construction is quite intricate, with several sections of hook-and-eye fastenings. Beige brocade patterned with garlands of pink and blue roses enhanced with green leaves underlays sections of yellow silk faille. The floor-length gown has a short train of brocade and silk faille. The three-quarter-length sleeves are floral brocade ending with poufs of yellow silk. Adorning the hip areas and below are elaborate sections of gold braid with metal spiral pendants in green, blue, silver, and bronze colors falling freely.

Mrs. Beaver's gown is one of a dozen pieces of costume from former first ladies of the commonwealth that are in the collection of The State Museum. Such textiles are kept in a specially refrigerated storage area for preservation purposes. This gown provides information not only about the fabrics and construction techniques of the period, but also about the formality of the clothing worn to political celebrations.

CARVED HUMAN EFFIGY

This carved steatite human effigy was found by Gerald B. Fenstermaker at the Keller Site in Washington Boro and sold to The State Museum of Pennsylvania in 1929. The Keller Site is associated with the Washington Boro Village Site, a Susquehannock town dating to c.1600–1625. The purpose of the effigy is not known. The artifact is particularly significant because it demonstrates a hairstyle likely worn by the Susquehannock people. It is 3.75 inches tall, 1.5 inches wide, and .5 inch thick.

SUSQUEHANNOCK POTTERY VESSEL

This clay pot, referred to as a Washington Boro incised pottery vessel, was found by Gerald B. Fenstermaker at the same site as the carved human effigy and sold to The State Museum in 1929. The vessel is typical of pottery made by the Susquehannocks during this period. It is made of local clay tempered with crushed mussel shell. The pronounced collar bears incised decorations and human effigy faces. The body is marked with impressions of a cordwrapped paddle.

The elaborate decoration of this vessel, 5 inches tall and 4.75 inches in diameter, represents the high point of the Susquehannock pottery-making tradition. As a result of greater trade with Europeans and the resulting increased use of metal kettles, later Susquehannock pottery is plainly decorated and not as well made.

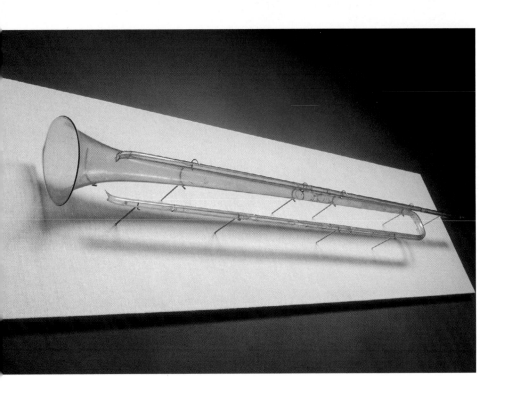

EIGHTEENTH-CENTURY GLASS TRUMPET

This rare three-foot-long glass trumpet was discovered at the Ephrata Cloister historic site in Lancaster County by a State Museum of Pennsylvania archaeological field school in the summer of 1995. It mimics "natural" trumpets (trumpets with no valves or slides) made of brass or silver in the sixteenth to eighteenth centuries. The artifact was found in a refuse pit dating to c. 1732–35.

Ephrata Cloister was a religious communal society that emphasized self-denial and separation from the outside world. The society had no instrumental music tradition, hence the trumpet's appearance at Ephrata is a mystery. Its maker and place of manufacture are unknown. The object is an extraordinary example of glass art and is the only one of its kind ever found in North America.

RUFFED GROUSE

The ruffed grouse (*Bonasa umbellus*) is the state bird of Pennsylvania. Less common today than historically, this bird is most abundant in forests having extensive ground cover or understory. Males of this handsome species beat their wings, called drumming, to attract mates during the spring.

The circle of black feathers around its neck gives the bird its name. When a male bird is defending his territory or trying to attract a hen, these feathers are extended into a spectacular ruff, which, together with his fanned-out tail, make him look twice his actual size.

Most ruffed grouse in Pennsylvania are patterned with a brown tail and black band, but some individuals have gray tails, and still fewer are found with an overall reddish hue, brown ruff, and brown tailband.

WHITE-TAILED DEER

The white-tailed deer (*Odocoileus virginianus*) is the state game animal of Pennsylvania. Although it is hard to believe today, this species was nearly extinct in the early twentieth century. White-tailed deer are common now in fields and forests; hunting is carefully regulated in the state.

Partially leucistic or piebald individuals, such as this one, are uncommon. Because this color pattern makes them stand out to predators, most individuals of this type do not survive past young adulthood.

TRILOBITE FOSSIL

The Pennsylvania state fossil, formerly known as *Phacops rana*, received a new name, *Eldredgeops rana*, in 1990 to honor the well-known invertebrate paleontologist Niles Eldredge. *Eldredgeops rana* is a small trilobite, measuring up to 1 inch in length.

Trilobites are extinct marine arthropods, part of a group that includes crabs, lobsters, spiders, horseshoe crabs, millipedes, centipedes, and insects. They are characterized by having a head, usually with large compound eyes; main body segment, or thorax; and tail, or pygidium. The name trilobite refers to the creature's three lengthwise lobes, one central and two lateral (axial). Trilobites lived on the ocean floor and were abundant during the early part of the Paleozoic Era, 570 to 245 million years ago. *Eldredgeops rana* was common on the East Coast of North America, particularly New York and Pennsylvania, during the middle Devonian Period, 386 to 377 million years ago.

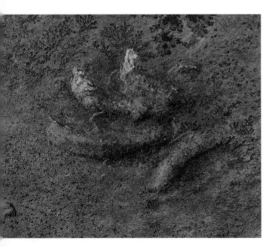

TRIASSIC REPTILE FOOTPRINT

This tiny reptile footprint was made by a small, lizardlike creature that lived during the Late Triassic Period, 235 to 208 million years ago. Paleontologists called these fossil footprints *Rhynchosauroides*; they have been found in North America and Europe. The skeletal remains of the small reptile that created the footprints have never been recognized, so the identity of the animal remains a mystery.

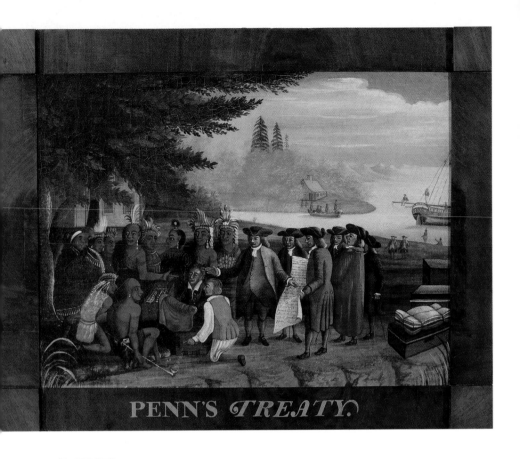

PENN'S TREATY.

PENN'S TREATY

When William Penn's son Thomas, living in London, commissioned the Pennsylvania-born artist Benjamin West in 1771 to create a painting memorializing his father's radical, lofty desire for Europeans and Native Americans to lead a "kind, just and peaceable life," nearly a century had passed since the elder Penn had founded Pennsylvania, his "holy experiment." West's painting, *William Penn's Treaty with the Indians When He Founded the Province of Pennsylvania in North America*, became known here and abroad through prints and books, inspiring later generations of artists.

One such artist was the nineteenth-century American folk painter Edward Hicks (1780–1849). A Quaker like

Penn, Hicks is perhaps best known for his series of *Peaceable Kingdoms*, which often include a Penn Treaty vignette. Shown here is Hicks's c. 1830 *Penn's Treaty*. The 17.25-by-23.25-inch oil painting in a block frame of mahogany veneer is the seminal work in The State Museum's Penn Treaty Collection. Donated to the museum by Meyer P. and Vivian O. Potamkin, the collection, dating from the eighteenth through the twentieth century, includes prints, ceramics, textiles, medals, books, and other memorabilia depicting images of Penn's efforts to treat native peoples with fairness. The collection clearly documents the popularity of this hopeful image of peace.

COLOR STUDY FOR *UNITY*

Violet Oakley (1874–1961) was the most important woman muralist of early-twentieth-century America. In 1902, she was chosen to create *The Holy Experiment*, large-scale murals for the governor's reception room in the new Pennsylvania State Capitol. At that time, it was the largest public commission ever entrusted to a woman. Later, Oakley also received commissions for murals in the chambers of the State Senate and the State Supreme Court.

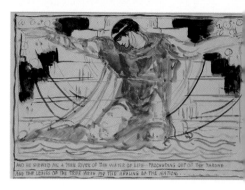

Believing that the artist's role was to teach and inspire, Oakley sought to express the history and principles of the commonwealth in her murals. She became an expert on the life and beliefs of William Penn. An activist and idealist, the artist regarded the Quaker doctrine of peace and personal freedom as the seeds from which Pennsylvania and the nation had grown and would progress.

For her murals, Oakley created preparatory sketches, drawings, and paintings in ink, charcoal, pencil, water- color, gouache, and oil. *Color Study, Unity, Senate Chamber, Pennsylvania State Capitol*, c. 1911, is a study for the heroic central figure in the senate chamber mural, representing the unity of all life. Oakley painted the allegorical female, Unity, in shades of blue, a color she used to symbolize wisdom. Executed in gouache, pencil, and ink on paper, the study measures fourteen by ten inches.

Some four hundred of Oakley's works were donated to The State Museum by the Violet Oakley Memorial Foundation. They provide important documentation of her creative process in developing the capitol murals.

TIN FIRE PUMPER TOY

This c. 1840 tin fire pumper, attributed to Francis, Field and Francis of Philadel- phia, is thought to be the earliest known manufactured American toy. Historians believe that the company, also known as the Philadelphia Tin Toy Manufactory, was the first toy manufacturer of record in the United States.

Francis, Field and Francis made toy horse-drawn carts, locomotives, an omnibus, and a boat called the *General Taylor*. The toy tin fire pumper surfaced in the 1980s and changed hands a few times before California collector and former Pennsylvania resident Lewis Leis donated it to The State Museum in 1999.

Only two other toys by Francis, Field and Francis are known to exist today. In addition to its rarity, the pumper underscores the importance of fire companies and firefighting in nine- teenth-century America. Remarkably, it retains most of its original painted dec- oration. Its rarity and condition elevate it from toy to treasure.

RABBIT CAROUSEL FIGURE

Manufactured by the Dentzel Carousel Company, this c. 1903 hand-carved Dentzel "flirting rabbit" was originally part of a fifty-four-figure carousel installed at Woodside Park in Philadelphia. The company, known for its fine craftsmanship, was considered one of the country's premier carousel makers.

The flirting rabbit also speaks to the fertile imagination of the company's lead carver, Salvatore Cernigliaro. Soon after joining Dentzel, the Sicilian-born immigrant ended the company's practice of carving from preset patterns. Cernigliaro's designs were intricately detailed and often included fancy straps, elaborate drapery, and whimsical embellishments such as cats with fish and rabbits with raised paws.

Dentzel's menagerie carousels were the company's most expensive. Today individual animals like this one are highly prized by collectors and museums alike.

History of The State Museum of Pennsylvania

The State Museum of Pennsylvania was founded in 1905 to preserve important historical objects and safeguard the commonwealth's material heritage. During its first century, the museum had to deal with various hurdles, numerous administrations, and changes in the museum world from an object orientation to a people-driven philosophy, as it challenged itself to define and fulfill its mission.

Early collection habits were oriented toward preservation of objects, not interpretation to the general public. Over time, the range and philosophy of collecting at The State Museum broadened from cabinets of curiosities to a more immersive environment that provides a learning experience on many topics to a wide range of visitors. This development continues today as The State Museum evaluates what it means to be a museum in the twenty-first century and how it can best serve its audiences.

From the mid-1800s on, art and artifacts had been donated to the state. The number of items increased after the Chicago World Columbian Exposition of 1893 and the Louisiana Purchase Exposition of 1904 in St. Louis, when exhibits were given to government agencies. State librarian Thomas Lynch Montgomery suggested a state museum to oversee these and other objects in Pennsylvania's custody.

Gov. Samuel Pennypacker signed Act 43 on March 28, 1905, officially creating The State Museum of Pennsylvania as part of the State Library for "the preservation of objects illustrating the flora and fauna of the state, and its mineralogy, geology, archaeology, arts, and history." Initial funding was $20,000. Montgomery kept his job as librarian and also became director of the museum. When the new Pennsylvania State Capitol was dedicated in October 1906, the governor and other officials vacated their offices in the Executive Office Building, and in 1907 museum staff moved in.

The museum's first two divisions were Education and Zoology, which included the collections of archaeology and geology. Holdings grew through donations from Pennsylvania's Game

William Penn, founder and first proprietor of Pennsylvania, is honored in the museum's Memorial Hall by an eighteen-foot-high bronze statue by sculptor Janet de Coux.

Interior of the State Library and Executive Building, first home of The State Museum, in 1921. PENNSYLVANIA STATE ARCHIVES

Commission, Fish Commission, and Department of Agriculture, among others. In 1906, the museum received twenty-five hundred stone tools for its archaeological collection.

Montgomery, Education Division curator Alicia Zierden, and Zoology Division curator Boyd P. Rothrock were early members of the American Association of Museums (AAM), founded in 1906. Topics of discussion at AAM meetings included technical issues such as how to hang and label exhibits (labeling was in its infancy then) and provided the opportunity to share ideas. The curators worked to make sure The State Museum followed professional standards of the day.

The Education Division presented the museum's first exhibition in April 1908. Educational and social economy items from the Louisiana Purchase Exhibition of 1904 were the core of the exhibit, supplemented by artwork created by schoolchildren across the state.

Also in 1908, the Lantern Slides Division was created. Weekly lectures at the museum, on topics from historic sites to ornithology to industry, were illustrated with slide shows. The division also made lantern slides available for schools to borrow. The collection grew to more than thirteen thousand slides in 1912 and one hundred thousand by the early 1940s.

The museum's growth was gradual. The History Division was founded in 1909, followed by the Geology Division in 1913. In Zoology, Rothrock amassed more than five hundred specimens. He traveled to other museums to learn cutting-edge mounting and display techniques. Large glass-window cases, similar to those of department stores fronted the presentations.

With the United States' 1917 entry into World War I, staff dwindled; new lighting went unused because of constraints on the use of electricity; and lantern slide circulation dipped because of national restrictions on entertainment.

LANTERN SLIDES

Lantern slides, introduced in 1849, allowed photographs to be projected and viewed by a large audience, making the medium appropriate for entertainment and education. Philadelphia brothers William and Frederick Langenheim developed transparent images that could be projected, unlike opaque daguerreotypes, by adhering a light-sensitive solution onto glass to create a negative, then using the negative to print onto another sheet of glass. This gave a positive image.

Original projectors used oil lamps. These were replaced by limelight, oxygen and hydrogen burned on a lime pellet, which gave way to carbon arc lamps and ultimately electric lights.

The development of the Kodachrome three-color process allowed 35-millimeter film slides to be produced more cheaply than glass slides, rendering the older technology obsolete. The State Museum's lantern slide collection is in the Pennsylvania State Archives.

Lantern Slides were an important educational tool in the early years of the museum. The slide above shows Market Street in Philadelphia. To the left is the Hiking Club of the Broad Street Branch of the YMCA in Harrisburg.

THE POSTWAR ROLLER COASTER
After World War I came a decade of ups and downs. The History Division was dissolved in 1919. In 1921, the museum had ten staffers, including an assistant taxidermist, two lantern slide assistants, and a foliage fabricator. Two years later, Gov. Gifford Pinchot transferred the museum to the Department of Public Instruction (today Education), where it was a low priority and experienced inadequate financing and high staff turnover. By 1926, the staff was down to two people, director Anna A. McDonald and one curator, and there was no money to circulate lantern slides. When Frederick A. Godcharles took over in 1927, he secured more funding, and the staff increased to nine.

During all of this, exhibit content continued to diversify. In 1922, Susquehannock Indian archaeological specimens were obtained.

In 1928, the museum highlighted pioneer life, displayed artwork by Pennsylvania poet and painter Lloyd Mifflin, and set up forty-eight glass cases in the rotunda, filling them with museum artifacts. Henry K. Deisher, who had sold a collection of archaeological specimens to the museum and become a volunteer, was hired as an assistant curator and implemented a sorely needed cataloging system. On the second floor, staffers painted backgrounds, prepared specimens for mounting, and opened the Animal Room in 1929. A series of large paintings by Peter F. Rothermel chronicling the Battle of Gettysburg were installed.

Visitation during this period was gratifying. In 1929, the AAM ranked the Pennsylvania State Museum as one of the top sixteen museums in the country, boasting a total annual attendance of more than twenty thousand, including many schoolchildren.

But the museum again suffered during the Depression. Staff was reduced from twelve to three between 1931 and 1933. Spending was slashed from $250,000 in 1929 to $185,000 in 1935.

The State Museum became an important community center in the 1940s.

In the 1930s, exhibitions emphasized cultural history and technology, including Pennsylvania-born authors, the progression of home heating, and notable Pennsylvania women. Five Pennsylvania Constitutions were put on display. The museum acquired a Colonial forge, cider press, sleighs, wheeled vehicles, and Conestoga wagons. The archaeology collection continued to grow, with a fifteen-thousand-piece collection of Native American artifacts and the Safe Harbor petroglyphs, rescued from the field in Lancaster County before being submerged by the construction of a new dam.

In 1938, two projects were funded by money from the Works Progress Administration (WPA), established by the Roosevelt administration to create jobs. One was to repair and clean animal exhibits; the other was to create lantern slides, dioramas, costume plates, paintings of wildflowers, geological models, and maps.

MIDCENTURY METAMORPHOSIS
In the 1940s and 1950s, the museum also became a community center where people came for classes, music rehearsals, and entertainment. When the United States entered World War II, the AAM joined in the patriotic efforts, recommending that its members sponsor exhibits and programs to entertain armed forces personnel. To that end, The State Museum added curator lectures, traveling exhibits, orientation sessions, and group tours. Military troops in Harrisburg-area camps were part of the new audience. The museum opened on Sundays, with attendance up to four thousand on those days for programs including live and recorded music and lantern slide shows about countries involved in the war.

Another major event, in 1944, was the three-hundredth anniversary of William Penn's birth, for which celebrations were held statewide. The Penn Charter and other archival documents were displayed in The State Museum. People began to question why there was no monument to Penn in Harrisburg. One group lobbied for the erection of a memorial, while state archivists articulated the need to preserve documents such as the Penn Charter.

On June 1, 1945, the General Assembly decreed that the state erect "a memorial building to honor the memory of William Penn, and other necessary buildings for the state archives, library and museum." Five days later, Gov. Edward Martin signed an act combining The State Museum, State Archives, and Historical Commission into the Pennsylvania Historical and Museum Commission (PHMC). This was the most significant development affecting the museum in the mid-twentieth century, continuing the museum's mandate to preserve, interpret, and celebrate Pennsylvania history.

Space had become a problem, as the museum shared its building with other state agencies and had to rent storage space in other buildings. Around this time, the museum was able to gain control of the building and brought back its items that had been off-site, stimulating a reorganization of the departments into Natural History, Earth Science, Entomology, Folk History, Photography, Archaeology, Preparation, and Shop.

The 1950s saw the adoption of a four-objective museum policy drafted by chief curator Kenneth Dearoff: tell a continuous story of Pennsylvania history; achieve a high standard of exhibit quality; present a balanced and properly proportioned amount of material; and

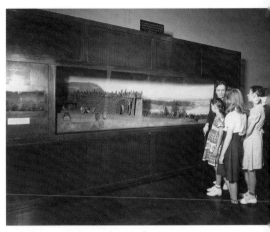

Dioramas were popular in the museum exhibitions of the 1950s.

always have temporary and changing exhibits to keep something new before the public. Dioramas were used more frequently, portraying the Battle of Germantown, the Battle of Lake Erie, Canal Days at New Hope, and the 28th Division passing under Paris's Arc de Triomphe in World War II. Costumed docents interpreted a country store exhibit for the public. The museum created a popular exhibit for the Pennsylvania Farm Show in 1952 depicting a Colonial riflemaking shop, and a dairy industry display the following year.

A NEW HOME
The three hundredth anniversary of William Penn's birth was the first step in a twenty-year journey that culminated in a new museum building. A Washington, D.C., based group called the Pennsylvania Historical Junta, spearheaded by historian Homer T. Rosenberger, had a large Capitol Park Penn monument in mind. The effort went nowhere in the Capitol Extension project. PHMC's executive director, Sylvester K. Stevens, suggested that a new Archives Building could

William Penn Memorial Museum and Archives Building. *This architect's rendering of the third home of the museum, renamed to honor Pennsylvania's founder. The name was changed back to The State Museum in the 1980s to reflect the broad scope of its holdings.*

include a statue of William Penn, but Rosenberger insisted on a separate statue. Later, Stevens added the museum to the mix of archives and memorial.

Governor Martin had given his support to a William Penn Memorial Museum and Archives Building, and a PHMC committee began to plan for a new structure. Architect William Gehron drafted plans for the building even before the sites were completely surveyed. But Martin's successor, James H. Duff, considered it a low priority, and funding was diverted. Nevertheless, the PHMC kept lobbying for a new building.

Stevens worked tirelessly to make the William Penn Memorial Museum and Archives Building a reality. He initiated Operation Heritage to educate Pennsylvanians about the PHMC's objectives and prepared a leaflet describing the need for a new structure, citing

overcrowded exhibit groupings and storage, a lack of heat and humidity control, dangerous electrical circuitry, and lack of fireproofing. There wasn't even enough room to store paintings that had been borrowed by earlier governors; when Governor George M. Leader wanted to give them back, he was turned down.

Finally the General Assembly was convinced. In April 1957, a resolution authorized money for the project. The firm of Lawrie & Green completed the architectural plans. Stevens turned to state historical societies to support construction appropriations and pressure the governor and legislature. These efforts paid off. The bill allocating $11 million passed the legislature and was signed into law by Gov. David L. Lawrence on December 29, 1959.

The new building would provide the opportunity for The State Museum to give Pennsylvania "back to the people," said Governor Lawrence. New display techniques, educational methods, and technology would be used to their fullest potential. The building's other impetus, creating a memorial to William Penn, would be realized in Memorial Hall, a shrine to Pennsylvania's founder.

Starting in 1960, staffers identified, stored, and packed thousands of artifacts. Construction contracts were awarded for the William Penn Memorial Museum and Archives at 300 North Street. Ground was broken on January 23, 1962.

The building's uncluttered exterior is emblematic of midcentury Modern design. Its distinct circular shape earned it the nickname "Central Pennsylvania Guggenheim," a tongue-in-cheek allusion to Manhattan's Modernist icon. Supposedly, provisions were made for staff and visitor parking, but the space was expropriated for office space instead.

Inside, Memorial Hall's fifty-six-foot-high rotunda is flanked by mezzanines on the second and third floors. Facsimilies of important documents are displayed around the perimeter of the first floor. Anchoring the space is a thirty-eight-hundred-pound bronze statue of William Penn by Pennsylvania sculptor Janet de Coux. Vincent Maragliotti's ninety-by-twenty-four-foot mural depicting the history of Pennsylvania and William Penn's ideals surrounds one end of the hall. Charles Rudy created Memorial Hall's massive bronze gates, ornamented with figures of memorable Pennsylvanians.

On May 20, 1964, Gov. William W. Scranton presided over the date stone dedication ceremony. The public got a sneak peek at the museum in December of that year. The William Penn Memorial Museum opened in April 1965 as the country's largest state museum, but it was almost empty. Memorial Hall was open, transportation exhibits were displayed in the ground-level and museum plaza windows, and a few temporary exhibits on the ground floor gave a taste of things to come. But that was it. Visitors would have to be patient as galleries opened one by one over the next several years.

THE MUSEUM EXPANDS ITS OFFERINGS

Construction and opening of major galleries and halls took place over the first fifteen years in the new building, melding scholarship, museum professionalism, administrative tasks, funding, and a dedicated labor force. Collections grew, educational programs flourished, and the museum's image became one of greater diversity, using many materials and formats to deliver exhibit storylines.

The museum was officially dedicated on October 13, 1965. On the twenty-first, the Fine Arts Gallery opened. "N. C. Wyeth and the Brandywine Tradition" drew more than forty thousand visitors before it closed in late November. The Planetarium also opened in 1965. Beginning in 1966, visitors could also enjoy the gift shop, entertainment programs, and holiday celebrations. What later became known as the "Art of the State" annual juried exhibit began in 1967. In the late 1960s, a Mobile Museum took to the road.

Mammal Hall, dioramas filled with Pennsylvania animals, opened in 1968. The Hall of Industry and Technology followed in 1971. The Hall of Natural Science, or Ecology Hall, had a 1973 opening with special guest Smokey Bear. Anthropology and Archaeology Hall, which includes cultural history and ethnology, was dedicated in 1975; Geology Hall, which introduces visitors to Penn-

Mobile Museum. From the late 1960s through 1995, portable exhibits from The State Museum toured Pennsylvania.

sylvania's geology, paleontology, paleobotany, and mineralogy, in 1976.

As galleries opened, the Education Division also evolved. The museum staff began to teach more, designed programs for young people, including a science fair and a history festival, and reached out to special-needs students and groups.

The State Museum of Pennsylvania received accreditation from the AAM in 1978, an indication of its dedication to professional standards and its standing in the museum community.

The year 1981 saw three Black History Month programs. Gradually, exhibits celebrating Martin Luther King Day became a Black History Month tradition.

A new nonprofit group, the Friends of the State Museum, was founded in 1982. The group ran the gift shop, gave holiday programs, presented a film series, and supported the museum's strategic planning and marketing efforts.

A NEW IDENTITY;
A RENEWED COMMITMENT

Its name led many people to believe that the William Penn Memorial Museum was devoted solely to Penn rather than encompassing so much more of relevance to Pennsylvania. In 1984, the PHMC approved a name change back to The State Museum of Pennsylvania.

The museum upheld its commitment to mirror the commonwealth's complexity. Donations, such as a chair made from Penn's treaty elm, studies for the Pennsylvania Capitol murals by Violet Oakley, a 1948 Packard, 1860 presentation silver, and invertebrate fossils enhanced the collections.

When Carl Nold became director in 1984, he focused on changing exhibits. During the 1987–88 holiday season, the museum offered "Christmas . . . An Ethnic Experience." The museum began to handle blockbuster exhibits, starting with "The Dinosaurs" in 1988. More than 103,000 people enjoyed the exhibit and events during its eight-week run.

In July 1990, the museum mounted its largest temporary exhibition: "Pennsylvania's New Deal: Jobs, Art, and Politics." That same month, PHMC director Brent D. Glass reorganized the commission, making The State Museum a separate bureau from the Bureau of Historic Sites and Museums.

Anita Blackaby took over as museum director in 1992, and public programming continued to flourish, including the well-received "Highlights Tour," a major history exhibit called "Discovering America: The Peoples of Pennsylvania," and "Winter Whimsies," which showed traditional crafters working. The Education Division launched "mini-lessons" to increase visitors' hands-on experience and interaction with staff, offered popular archaeology workshops, and set up "Stop and Learn" stations throughout the museum. Dino Lab, an area where visitors watch and interact with preparators working on dinosaur fossils, opened in 1993.

The museum continued to receive significant donations, including the Penn Treaty Collection from Mr. and Mrs. Meyer P. Potamkin in 1995 and 1996, which consists of 109 pieces of art and objects with the image of William Penn's treaty with the Indians.

Throughout the 1990s, the museum focused on social and ethnic history, young people, and fine arts. It featured series on civil rights and on the Latino experience in the state, and addressed issues such as bullying and prejudice. As part of the social history focus, the Decorative Arts section was renamed Community and Domestic Life in 1994. Here, folk art and objects used by working-class people took their place alongside fancy parlor furniture. A new curatorial section called Popular Culture opened in 1999. In this section of the museum, objects from white, upper-class eighteenth- and nineteenth-century people were supplemented with artifacts that reflected the experience of ordinary people in their daily lives.

From 2000 through 2004, The State Museum moved a number of curatorial offices and science collections to the new Commonwealth Keystone Building. The first phase of museum renovations began in 2002. The year 2004 was notable for the opening of Curiosity Connection, a hands-on learning and play space for the museum's youngest visitors.

ONE HUNDRED YEARS AND BEYOND

As The State Museum of Pennsylvania begins its second hundred years, it is constantly in transition, facing new challenges and taking advantage of new opportunities. This visitor-centered, socially responsible institution continues the cycle of change that began in the museum world by the 1980s.

The museum has been updating and upgrading its spaces and programs, welcoming visitors with a new reception desk evocative of William Penn's boat, the *Welcome*. A digital planetarium system now gives more options on what visitors can experience. The collections are still evolving as well. What began as an assemblage of precious or rare items now also includes ordinary things like Tupperware because of their relevance to everyday life.

Nearly three hundred thousand visitors each year enjoy special events and activities, including Heritage Week, fall and spring educational programs, and summer workshops. An important exhibition, "Flight 93 Remembered," displayed items that visitors left in memory of those who lost their lives on September 11, 2001, in Schenksville, Somerset County. During the exhibit's first weekend, more than nine hundred people visited the museum.

The staff actively conducts research and offers educational programs, a website, and in-house demonstrations.

Although it is a venerable institution, The State Museum of Pennsylvania remains dynamic and alive, a meaningful destination for all Pennsylvanians.

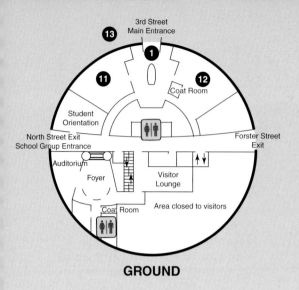

GROUND

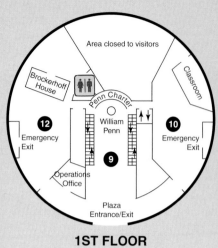

1ST FLOOR

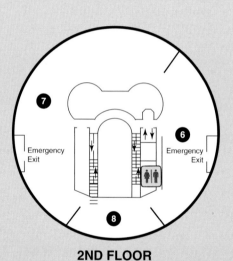

2ND FLOOR

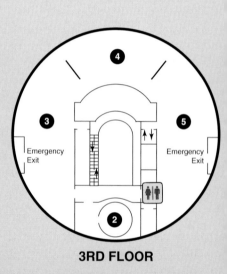

3RD FLOOR

MUSEUM LEGEND

1 Information Desk

2 Planetarium

3 Hall of Paleontology and Geology

4 Mammal Hall

5 Hall of Natural Science and Ecology

6 Hall of Anthropology and Archaeology

7 Hall of Industry and Technology

8 Civil War Gallery

9 Memorial Hall

10 Market, Shop, and Home

11 Curiosity Connection

12 Changing Exhibits

13 Exterior

🚻 Restrooms

Visiting the Museum

INFORMATION DESK

Visitors entering the museum are greeted at an information desk that resembles William Penn's ship, the *Welcome*. Here is the place to obtain a site map, ask questions, and buy tickets for "Curiosity Connection" or planetarium shows. Admission to The State Museum of Pennsylvania is free; however, a fee is charged for planetarium shows and "Curiosity Connection." A coatroom, museum shop, ATM, auditorium, restrooms, and vending machines are also located here on the ground floor.

After entering the museum, most visitors go up to the third floor and work their way back down.

PLANETARIUM

A new concept in planetarium projection, called the digital planetarium, was introduced in the spring of 2005, replacing all the slide projectors and special effects used in a conventional planetarium. This technology can create a changing star field, make visitors feel as though they are in a spaceship on a journey from earth to another planet, examine the constellations as they look from a backyard, zoom in on distant objects that are invisible to the naked eye, or project dome video shows, which use the whole dome to explore the planets, outer space, or such things as ancient Egyptian temples. Planetarium shows change regularly.

HALL OF PALEONTOLOGY AND GEOLOGY

The Hall of Paleontology and Geology explores the history and diversity of life on earth. Visitors can take a walk through geologic time to discover some of the life forms that once inhabited Pennsylvania and see a collection of rocks and minerals.

Highlights include the large, prehistoric armored fish *Dunkleosteus terrelli*, the denizen of the deep that swam in the seas of Ohio and Pennsylvania about 367 million years ago. The Carbonifer-

ous Forest includes plants and animals of the Pennsylvanian Period, 310 million years ago. The Marshalls Creek Mastodont is a prehistoric elephant that lived in Pennsylvania during the Ice Age. Radiocarbon dating of wood samples from the Monroe County site indicate that the animal died approximately 12,000 years ago.

Dino Lab treats visitors to an insider's look at how museum fossil preparators work. This exhibit station is actually a laboratory in a gallery setting. While a technician painstakingly works to reveal dinosaur bones in sedimentary rock found in New Mexico, visitors can observe and ask questions. A camera zooms in on the technician's hands, showing how dental-type tools are used to gently excavate the skeletons.

4 MAMMAL HALL

A perennial favorite, Mammal Hall contains thirteen full-scale dioramas that dramatically illustrate Pennsylvania wildlife. The animals are depicted in their natural environments, engaged in behaviors such as finding food, caring for their young, and creating their homes.

Planning for Mammal Hall began around 1960. The museum slowly acquired the specimen mounts from natural science professionals and government agencies. Naturalists and artists made field trips to photograph, sketch, and observe the animals' habitats; they also brought back plants and materials for replication or inclusion in the dioramas.

Artist and preparator John Kucera was chiefly responsible for the artistic planning and construction. He and John Schreffler painted ten of the

backgrounds, and Jerome Connolly painted the other three. For the foregrounds, four people spent three years meticulously constructing artificial plant material.

Finally the animals, backgrounds, and foregrounds were merged, and Mammal Hall opened in 1968. From the striped skunk to the black bear, Pennsylvania's animals are realistically showcased in

their natural habitats, depicting variations in seasons, weather conditions, and behaviors. Techniques such as the use of varnish to make "water" appear wet add to the authenticity.

A major restoration of Mammal Hall was done in the early 1990s. Large windows extend almost to the floor, making the animals visible to even the tiniest tot.

⑤ HALL OF NATURAL SCIENCE AND ECOLOGY

Pennsylvania's seven ecosystems—mountain stream, lowland stream, lake/pond, bog, freshwater marsh, meadow/old field, and forest—are presented in terms of their rocks and minerals, water supply, plants, and animals. The logical progression shows how one ecosystem transforms into another, and the exhibits examine the features that characterize each. Snakes, colorful birds, beetles, bugs, fish, and native plants are displayed and interpreted, with emphasis on their relationships with each other and their environment.

6 HALL OF ANTHROPOLOGY AND ARCHAEOLOGY

Who were the first Pennsylvanians? Where did they come from? How did they live? Few written records exist to answer these questions, but archaeological evidence of these early inhabitants is rich, and it is presented and interpreted in this gallery.

The Hall of Anthropology and Archaeology gives a life-size view of what goes on at an archaeological dig and displays hundreds of Native American artifacts, including stone and clay pipes, throwing sticks, and cooking utensils. Exhibits trace the evolution of Native American culture from the retreat of the North American ice sheet to the first contact with Europeans. A replica of a Delaware Indian village offers a walk-through of the life of a Lenape Indian from birth to burial.

7 HALL OF INDUSTRY AND TECHNOLOGY

Progress and power characterize this gallery, which catalogs Pennsylvania's shift from a farming to an industrial society. Stagecoaches and Conestoga wagons, trains and trolleys, fire engines, a motorcycle, and airplanes chart Pennsylvania's transportation developments. The gallery looks at the changes from hand tools to steam engines and beyond.

Tools of the trade, including those used to saw wood, frame a barn, and build a house, offer a lively picture of Pennsylvania's past. An exhibit on textile development shows the shearing, carding, and spinning that once was necessary for making clothes.

Other exhibits tell the stories of the industrial uses for charcoal, coal, iron, and steel. Steam engines and an electrical turbine are on display, as well as a model coke factory. Improvements in lighting, from fat-burning lamps to electrical bulbs, vividly illustrate technological progress.

8 **CIVIL WAR GALLERY**

Evoking a time when brother fought brother, the Civil War Gallery includes objects and artifacts that recount the role of Pennsylvanians in the war: uniforms and accoutrements, medals, badges, canteens, guidons, drums, cartridges and shells, cannon, small arms, swords, and paintings. One of the presentation swords was manufactured by the New York jewelry firm catering to the country's carriage trade, Tiffany & Company. Colors, or flags, of several units are also on exhibit, including those carried by the Ringgold Light Artillery of Reading, the Logan Guards of Lewistown, and the 2nd Infantry Regiment of U.S. Colored Troops.

Paintings include *The Battle of Gettysburg: Pickett's Charge*, a monumental rendering of one of the fiercest battles in history. In 1866, Pennsylvania native Peter Frederick Rothermel (1812–95) was commissioned by the state legislature to do a series of Civil War paintings; *Pickett's Charge* is the largest. The artist took three years to transpose the drama of the battle onto canvas; the painting was unveiled on December 20, 1870.

This huge work of art, measuring thirty-two feet long by more than sixteen feet high, serves as a dramatic backdrop for the gallery. Rothermel, who created his masterpiece by synthesizing the collective memory of the many veterans he interviewed, grimly depicts courage in the face of horror and chaos. The painting is still capable of evoking deep emotions. A seven-minute video explains the battle and interprets the painting.

⑨ MEMORIAL HALL

The legacy of William Penn looms large at The State Museum of Pennsylvania, as does the statue of the commonwealth's founder as the centerpiece of Memorial Hall. The eighteen-foot-high, thirty-eight-hundred-pound bronze depicts a thoughtful, dignified, youthful countenance. The statue was created over a two-year period by Pittsburgh sculptor Janet de Coux for the building's opening in 1965. Nestled in Penn's left arm is a figure that represents all of humanity, with Penn as protector.

A reproduction of the Charter for Pennsylvania, granted by England's King Charles II to Penn, as well as a selection of documents basic to the foundation of the commonwealth also are displayed in Memorial Hall. The documents encased here are copies; the originals are stored in a climate-controlled archival vault in the adjacent State Archives.

An immense mural painted by Vincent Maragliotti depicts momentous events and important Pennsylvania individuals, with the theme "William Penn's vision of a free society and what came out of it." Maragliotti began by making small black-and-white drawings, then converted them to full size. Next, he made colored sketches at the scale of a half inch to a foot and transferred them onto canvas, which he cut into sections. He made a slide of each section, projected these onto the full-size canvas, and traced the outlines with charcoal. Maragliotti then used specially treated oil paint to create a fresco effect.

Also notable in Memorial Hall are the bronze ornamental gates adorned with important Pennsylvanians, created by Bucks County artist Charles Rudy.

⑩ MARKET, SHOP, AND HOME

A re-created nineteenth-century village takes visitors to a street from long ago, where merchants and artisans made and sold their wares. A hardware store, general store, and chair shop are among the extensively outfitted areas along the cobblestone lane.